My Path to Math

WHAT COMES IN SETS?

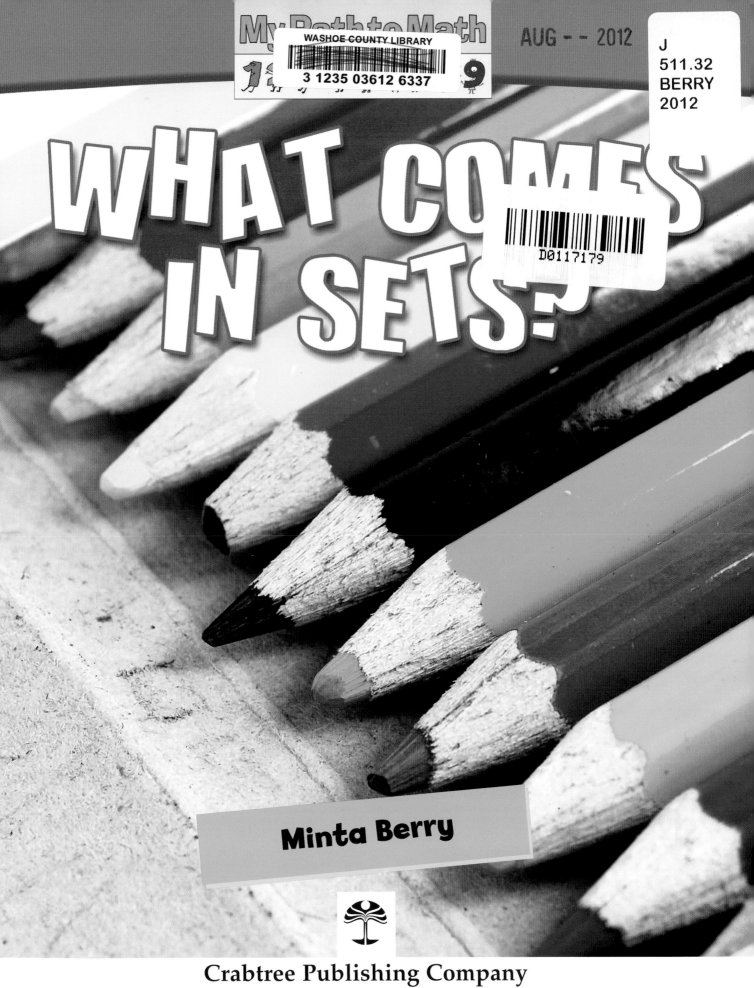

Minta Berry

Crabtree Publishing Company
www.crabtreebooks.com

Author: Minta Berry
Editor: Reagan Miller
Publishing plan research and development:
    Sean Charlebois, Reagan Miller
    Crabtree Publishing Company
Proofreader: Crystal Sikkens
Cover design: Margaret Amy Salter
Editorial director: Kathy Middleton
Production coordinator: Margaret Amy Salter
Prepress technician: Margaret Amy Salter
Print coordinator: Katherine Berti
Project manager: Kirsten Holm, Shivi Sharma (Planman Technologies)
Photo research: Iti Shrotriya (Planman Technologies)
Technical art: Arka Roy Chaudhary (Planman Technologies)

Photographs: Cover: Felix Mizioznikov/Shutterstock; P4: (tl)
PhotoHappiness/Shutterstock; (tc) PhotoHappiness/Shutterstock; (tr)
4ever.Rik/Shutterstock; (b) Ralf Neumann/Shutterstock; P5: (bkgd.toys)
Mdmfotos/123RF, (fgd.girl) Jaimie Duplass/Shutterstock; P6: (t) Julián
Rovagnati/Shutterstock, (c.t) Smit/Shutterstock, (c.b) Eugen Wais/Shutterstock;
(b) Analia Valeria Urani/Shutterstock; P7: (t) Monkey Business
Images/Shutterstock; (b.bkgd.paper) Jackiso/Shutterstock; P8 (t)
Anetta/Shutterstock; (c.l.) Robert Morton Photographs/IStockPhoto; (c.r.)
Ericmichaud/IStockPhoto; (b.bkgd.paper) Jackiso/Shutterstock, (b.fgd.button)
Picsfive/Shutterstock, (b.fgd.leaf) Smit/Shutterstock; P9: (tl.l) Artpose Adam
Borkowski/ Shutterstock, (tl.c) David Philips/Shutterstock, (tl.r) Todd
Taulman/ Shutterstock; (tr) Ljupco Smokovski/Shutterstock; (bl)
Vtldtlm/Shutterstock; (br.l) IstockPhoto/Thinkstock, (br.c) Danny
Smythe/Shutterstock, (br.r) AlexAvich/Shutterstock; P10: (t.tl) Monkey
Business Images/Shutterstock, (t.tr) AISPIX/Shutterstock, (t.bl) AISPIX/
Shutterstock, (t.br) AISPIX/ Shutterstock; (b.tl) Vasiliy Koval/Shutterstock, (b.tr)
Eric Isselée/ Shutterstock, (b.b) Eric Isselée/Shutterstock; P11: Vladimirs
Koskins/ Shutterstock; P12: (t) Picsfive/Fotolia; (b) JaNell Golden/
Shutterstock; P14: (tl) Gregg Cerenzio/Shutterstock; (tr) JuSun/IStockPhoto; (bl)
LoopAll/ IStockPhoto; (bc) Igor Shypitsyn/IStockPhoto; (br) Alexandr
akarov/ Shutterstock; P15: (t) In-Finity/Shutterstock; (c) Ruslan Kudrin/
Shutterstock; (b) George Clerk/IStockPhoto, P16: (t) Core Pics/Fotolia; (bl)
Franck Boston/ Shutterstock; (br) IstockPhoto/Thinkstock; P17: (tl)
Linor/Shutterstock; (tr) Tom K!/Sutterstock; (cl) Gregg Cerenzio/ Shutterstock;
(cr) Gregg Cerenzio/ Shutterstock; (bl) Melissa King/ Shutterstock; (br) S-TS/
Shutterstock; P18: (tl) Nattika/Shutterstock; (tr) Alivepix/Shutterstock; (cl);
Tatiana Popova/ Shutterstock (cr) Germany Feng/Shutterstock; (bl)
Surabhi25/Shutterstock; (br) Dulce Rubia/ Shutterstock; P19: (tl) Skyline/
Shutterstock; (tr) Randomdigit/IStockPhoto; (c) VikaRayu/Shutterstock; (bl)
Nata Sdobnikova/Shutterstock; (br) Aleksandar Bunevski/Shutterstock; P23:
(tl) Smit/Shutterstock; (tr) Teerapun/Shutterstock; (c.tl) Michaela Stejskalova/
Shutterstock; (c.tr) JaNell Golden/Shutterstock; (c.bl) MikePanic/ IStockPhoto;
(c.br) Melissa King/Shutterstock; (b) Gregg Cerenzio/ Shutterstock.
(t = top, b = bottom, l = left, c= center, r = right, bkgd = background, fgd =
foreground, ct = center top, cb = center bottom, tl = top left; tr = top right; bl =
bottom left; br = bottom right, bc = bottom center)

Library and Archives Canada Cataloguing in Publication

Berry, Minta
     What comes in sets? / Minta Berry.

(My path to math)
Includes index.
Issued also in electronic formats.
ISBN 978-0-7787-5279-0 (bound).--ISBN 978-0-7787-5268-4 (pbk.)

     1. Set theory--Juvenile literature. I. Title. II. Series: My path to math

QA248.B475 2011   j511.3'22   C2011-906794-3

Library of Congress Cataloging-in-Publication Data

Berry, Minta.
    What comes in sets? / Minta Berry.
         p. cm. -- (My path to math)
    Includes index.
    ISBN 978-0-7787-5279-0 (reinforced library binding : alk. paper) --
ISBN 978-0-7787-5268-4 (pbk. : alk. paper) -- ISBN 978-1-4271-8809-0
(electronic pdf) -- ISBN 978-1-4271-9650-7 (electronic html)
    1. Set theory--Juvenile literature. I. Title.
QA40.5.B47 2012
511.3'2--dc23
                                              2011040391

Crabtree Publishing Company

Printed in the U.S.A./112011/JA20111018

www.crabtreebooks.com   1-800-387-7650

Published in Canada
Crabtree Publishing
616 Welland Ave.
St. Catharines, ON
L2M 5V6

Published in the United States
Crabtree Publishing
PMB 59051
350 Fifth Avenue, 59th Floor
New York, New York 10118

Published in the United Kingdom
Crabtree Publishing
Maritime House
Basin Road North, Hove
BN41 1WR

Published in Australia
Crabtree Publishing
3 Charles Street
Coburg North
VIC 3058

Contents

What Is a Set?

Anna helps fold her clothes. She matches her socks. Her socks make a **set** of two.

A set is a group of **objects** that are alike in some way. Objects can be things, numbers, or shapes. A sock is an object. Two socks make up a set.

Activity Box

Look at the train. What is the set? What are the objects? How many objects are in the set?

Anna has many stuffed animals.
The animals make up a set.

Sets of Two

Anna and Josie help Anna's mom make a cake. While they work they see some sets of two.

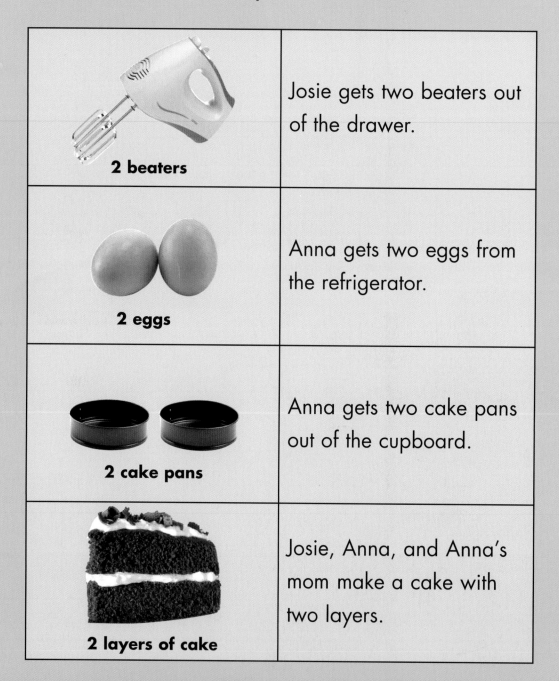

2 beaters	Josie gets two beaters out of the drawer.
2 eggs	Anna gets two eggs from the refrigerator.
2 cake pans	Anna gets two cake pans out of the cupboard.
2 layers of cake	Josie, Anna, and Anna's mom make a cake with two layers.

Anna and Josie are a set of two friends.

Activity Box

Look in the mirror. What parts of your body come in sets of two? Draw a picture of yourself. Make a list of the sets of two you have on you!

My Sets of Two

I have a set of two eyes.
I have a set of two _____ .

Sets of Three

Anna, Diego, and Aidan are playing outside. Help them find sets of three.

The tricycle has three wheels. The swing set has three red and yellow swings. The flower has three petals.

3 wheels

3 petals

Sets are not always objects. Breakfast, lunch, and dinner is a set of three. So is morning, noon, and night.

3 swings

Activity Box

Look at the picture. Make your own picture showing sets of three.

3

Anna and her friends play all day. They find more sets of three.

3 baseball bats

3 balls

3 sand tools

3 pieces of chalk

Sets of Four

Anna likes eating dinner with her family. Anna has a mother and father. She has a brother. His name is Mark. Her family makes a set of four.

family of 4

Anna's family has a cat, a dog, and two gerbils. Anna's pets are a set of four.

Anna sees many sets of four at the table.

4 saucers

4 cups

4 bowls

4 plates

4 chairs

Activity Box

Find the sets of four in the picture.

What sets of four did you find?

What other sets of four might go on the table?

Look in your home for a set of four.
Draw a picture of your set of four.

Sets of Five

Next, Anna looks for sets of five. She counts carefully. **Counting** helps Anna find the number of objects in a set.

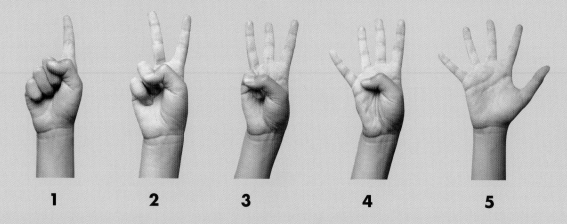

| 1 | 2 | 3 | 4 | 5 |

Anna sees that she has five fingers on one hand. Five fingers are a set of five.

Activity Box

Look at the picture. Use your fingers to point at each petal. How many petals are there?

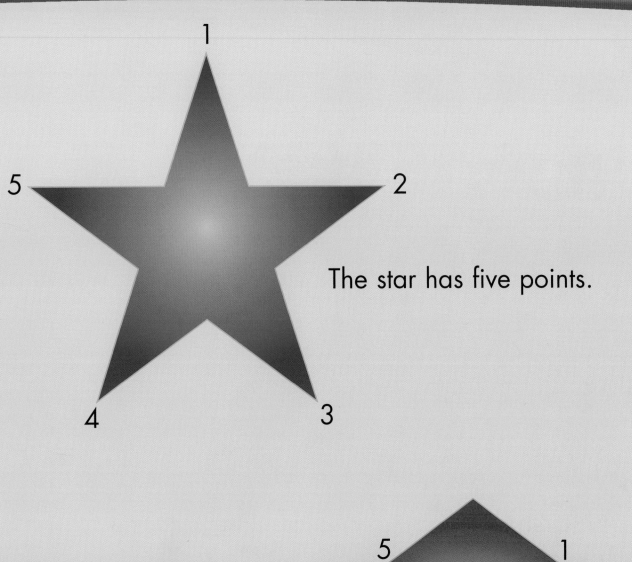

The star has five points.

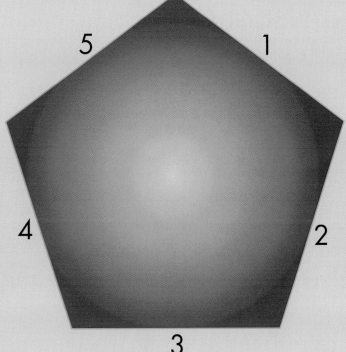

This shape is called a pentagon. A pentagon has five sides.

Bigger Sets

Anna likes looking for sets. She goes from room to room looking for more. She finds sets of six, seven, eight, nine, and ten.

6 eggs

CALENDAR

SUNDAY	MONDAY	TUESDAY	WEDNESDAY	THURSDAY	FRIDAY	SATURDAY
	1	2	3	4	5	6
7	8	9	10	11	12	13
14	15	16	17	18	19	20
21	22	23	24	25	26	27
28	29	30	31			

7 days in a week

Activity Box

Look at each picture. Count the number of objects in the set. Say the name of each number as you count.

Anna sees that sets can have any number of objects.

8 markers

9 bracelets

10 toes

Comparing Sets

Anna's friend Sam tells her that he can do more than count sets.

Sam shows Anna two trains. They count the train cars. One train has four cars. The other train has five cars.

Sam asks, "Which train has more cars?" Anna points to the train with five cars. She says, "The second train has **more than** the first."

Anna is **comparing** the two sets. She uses the words "more than" to say how they compare.

Activity Box

Count the fingers the boy is holding up. Then count the fingers the girl is holding up. Which set of fingers has more than the other?

Anna compares more sets. She counts the number of objects in each set. She uses the words more than, **less than**, or **equal to** when comparing the sets.

Six bananas is **more than** two bananas.

Six eggs is **less than** 12 eggs.

Ten fingers is **equal to** ten toes.

Comparing More Sets

Sam and Anna look around the house. They find more sets to compare.

Sam finds a set of three envelopes. Anna finds a set of four books. Anna's set of books is more than Sam's set of envelopes.

Anna finds a set of two tennis rackets. Sam finds a set of six golf clubs. Anna's set of tennis rackets is less than Sam's set of golf clubs.

Anna finds a set of two plums. Sam finds a set of two kiwis. Anna's set of plums is equal to Sam's set of kiwis.

Anna thinks she can find more sets than Sam.
Sam thinks he can find more sets than Anna.

Here are sets that Anna finds. | Here are sets that Sam finds.

a set of five keys

a set of three tennis balls

a set of four toothbrushes

a set of two sneakers

a set of two dumbbells

Did Anna or Sam find more sets?

Activity Box

Look around your house or your classroom.
What kinds of sets can you find?

Matching Sets

Anna's mother draws pictures on cards. Anna uses them to play a matching game with sets.

For the game, Anna takes a card and looks at the picture. Then she tries to find another card that will make a set.

First she chooses a card with one blue bird. What card could Anna choose to make a set?

She could choose a card with red birds. That would make a set of bird cards.

She could choose a card with one kite. That could make a set of cards with one object.

She could choose a card with blue flowers. That would make a set with blue objects.

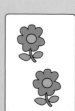

Anna lays out all the
cards on the table.
She looks for sets.

Activity Box

Now it is your turn to play the
game. Look at the cards above.
How many sets can you find?
Here are two sets.

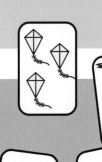

Glossary

comparing Telling how two sets are alike or different

counting Telling how many are in a set

equal to Two sets with the same number of objects

less than When a set is smaller than another set

more than When a set is larger than another set

objects Items in a set

set A group of objects that are alike in some way

Set of 2

Set of 3

Set of 4

Set of 5

Set of 6

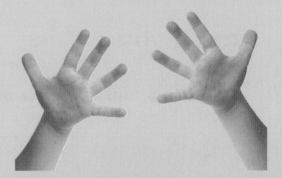

Set of 10

Set of 12

Index